Spiritual Wisdom Ignored
The Tragedy of America

When the powerless speak
truth and wisdom
And the powerful fail to listen,
All humanity suffers.

Patty Sue Patton

authorHOUSE®

AuthorHouse™
1663 Liberty Drive
Bloomington, IN 47403
www.authorhouse.com
Phone: 833-262-8899

Published by AuthorHouse 08/21/2020

ISBN: 978-1-4343-7092-1 (sc)

Library of Congress Control Number: 2008901764

Print information available on the last page.

Any people depicted in stock imagery provided by Getty Images are models, and such images are being used for illustrative purposes only. Certain stock imagery © Getty Images.

This book is printed on acid-free paper.

Special appreciation to my
husband of over 60 years:

Bob J. Tillerson
WWII Veteran and Retired Boy Scout Executive

whose love for nature and appreciation
for Native American history brought
me to the mountains of SW Colorado,
freeing both mind and soul to focus
on God's greatest gifts to all mankind.

Contents

Preface   xi

In The Beginning   1

Truth and Wisdom: Products of Spirituality   5

The Powerless Spoke but the Powerful Failed
    to Listen   7

Religion Comes to America   9

Churches in America   13

Spirituality in Another Part of the World   19

The Millennium, January 1, 2000   29

The Refugees   37

Dogmatic Beliefs Harm America   43

A New Gospel   49

The New Gospel and the Spirituality of
    Ancient People   57

Wise Folks, Great Accomplishments   65

Hope and Honor   69

Who Can Lead Us?   73

Summary   77

Epilogue   81

To My Readers   83

References   85

About the Author   87

List of Illustrations

The Gift, September 26, 1927   x

Chimney Rock Archaeological Site   2

Be Still and Know I Am God   46

Hand-Made doll made from corn husks   62

Hand-made doll in traditional clothing   63

Hand-made Kachina Doll   64

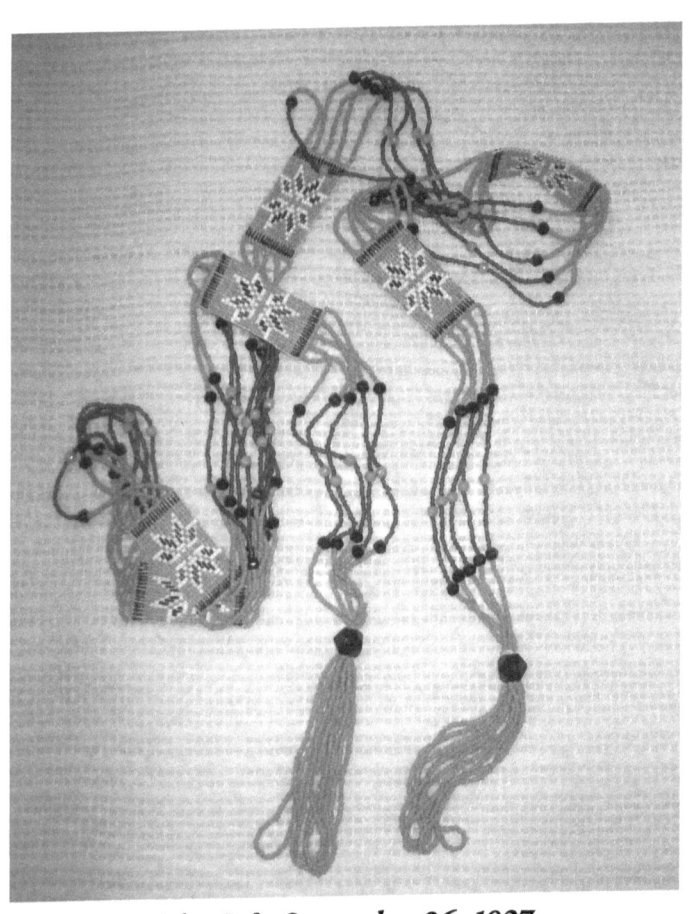

The Gift, September 26, 1927

Preface

As early as I can recall, I have felt an inner love for our original Americans, our Indian friends. It came to me during one of my morning walks, that perhaps this was planted when I was born in Muskogee, Oklahoma, located near the capitol of the Cherokee Nation, Tahlequah. The year was 1927. My father was in the bread business and he would donate his day-old bread to those folks to feed their hogs. He had a good relationship with them, one of respect.

When I was born, in honor of my birth, those kind folks presented to my father, a beautiful finely-beaded neck piece–very long, about 2 inches wide and 4 feet long, the kind one would drape around the neck and allow to flow down the front. I am sure this gift was presented as a blessing and my mother treasured it always. Today, it is safely "tucked away" in my grandmother's trunk of blessed memories.

My deep desire to learn more was finally realized during our retirement years when we moved to SW Colorado. Since that time, we have traveled the states and Canada and visited many different cultural centers to learn of the wisdom of those early tribal leaders, the original Americans. My writings focus on the tragic history of America when spiritual wisdom has been ignored both at home and abroad.

Patty Sue Patton Tillerson

In The Beginning

What was America like? It was a perfect creation of God.

To get an idea of what it must have been like for those original Americans, the first human inhabitants on this continent, let me suggest the following.

Set aside a night and a time when the stars will be out. Ask all your neighbors to join you in the celebration of creation. At the designated time, all lights, all TVs, all radios, all cell phones, all noises of our civilized life-style are silenced. Then go outside, in total darkness and silence, look up at the heavenly stars which, as stated in the "Thunder Moon" series, are the faces of the Sky People (God's angels) looking down on us. Listen to the sounds of creation–perhaps a dog barking, a horse neighing, an owl hooting – what an awesome experience!

Spiritual wisdom, planted in human brains by God, has been wrongly ignored when those in power failed to listen as expressed by the powerless in this way:

*I do not see a delegation for the four footed.
I see no seat for the Eagles. We forget and we
consider ourselves superior. But we are after
all a mere part of creation. And we must
consider to understand where we are. And
we stand somewhere between the mountain
and the ant. Somewhere and only there
is part and parcel of the creation. Oren
Lyons, Faithkeeper (National Museum of
the American Indian, pg 40)*

Chimney Rock Archaeological Site

There are many holy sites of the ancients around our country, many preserved and protected but many neglected. I am very proud that the holy site of Chimney Rock in SW Colorado is one that continues to be respected, protected, and preserved by volunteers living in that part of Colorado.

There are no developments close by, no huge souvenir centers or the such—all that is offered is the opportunity to appreciate the lives of those who lived there in the very early days of this land. No one knows why they abandoned the site, but it is speculated that it was due to drought and lack of water.

I had the privilege a few years ago to join a "Full Moon" guided tour. The nights of the Full Moon held spiritual significance to the ancients living there. Volunteers now protect the remains of their dwellings and allow no one to climb near the Chimney Rock itself. The tour takes folks to the highest place where the Full Moon can be seen rising from behind the Chimney as seen by the ancients. As I peered down into the valley below, it was as if I could see the spirits of the ancients dancing in the shadows, in praise for those who continue today to protect this holy site.

Truth and Wisdom: Products of Spirituality

Spirituality of our original Americans evolved from the beginning and continued throughout generations, stories handed down by their grandmothers and the wisdom of their tribal Chiefs and spiritual leaders. Their appreciation for all God had created was taught using the animal kingdom; the sun, moon and stars; the earth and all that grows to express their spirituality, their family values and their religious beliefs.

> *God gives his instructions to every creature, according to His plan for the world. He gave His instructions to all the things of nature. The pine tree and the birch tree, they still follow their instructions and do their duty in God's world. The flowers, even the littlest flower, they bloom and they pass away according to his instructions. The birds, even the smallest bird, they live and they fly and they sing according to His instructions. Should human beings be any*

> *different? Mathew King, Lakota wise man.*
> *(Native Universe, pg 83)*

Interestingly, childrens' books in our Western culture teach moral values through animal characters. Why is this? Children adore the animal world, the flowers, the rocks and leaves; are curious about the stars, the sun and the moon. Children too have God's instructions, given to each at the moment of life's first breath— a spiritual curiosity to discover their unique purpose for being here.

The Powerless Spoke
but the Powerful Failed to Listen

Let's leave our America for a little while and examine what was going on in the part of the world that did not know our land prior to 1492.

Among the discovery of the 2,000-year-old Dead Sea Scrolls in 1956, were the Qumran texts. Among them was a description of the beliefs and activities of the Essene community–a religious community prior to the birth of Christ. Of special fascination was the discovery of the words of the "greatest Commandment" as stated by Christ:

> Love the Lord your God with all your heart,
> with all your mind, and with all you soul
> and your neighbor as yourself.

This has led many scholars to wonder if perhaps Christian beliefs actually began with the Essenes. Manfred Barthel offers a more detailed account of this in his book, *What the Bible Really Says*. One thing is certain: history makes it apparent that those folks, at the time of Christ were the power*less,* whose wisdom went ignored since the life-style of the power*ful* was disdainful of spirituality and worship was centered on man-made images.

One only need compare that life-style with the spirituality of our original Americans to understand why God sent Christ to that part of the world. After all, God certainly knew about America–he created it! Obviously, the spiritual reverence of those Americans pleased God greatly.

The true message sent by God through Christ was that He is a God of love, not to be feared if only we accept and live by that greatest commandment:

> *Love the Lord your God*
> *With all your heart*
> *With all your mind*
> *With all your soul, and*
> *Your neighbor as yourself.*

But, what happened? The Power*ful* used the dogmatic interpretations of religion to subject those with spiritual wisdom to live in fear which included physical abuse, torture and even murder – all sanctioned by the religious power of the government.

The word "church" is found just twelve times in the Holy Bible and the word "organize" does not exist. Spirituality is spoken more than one-hundred times.

It appears that the church God intended is in each of us – our personal spirituality– to be discovered and lived!

Religion Comes to America

The Powerless came. The first immigrants of numbers included two types of immigrant groups. There were those who came for the opportunity to practice their religious beliefs without fear, and live in peace with each other.

They were hard-working, lived and practiced the "Great Commandment" and as a result, had no problems living in peace with the original Americans they encountered. They insisted that the Indian population be treated the same as all others; that their land be purchased rather than confiscated, and that none should ever be captured and used as slaves.

The other groups of immigrants, for the most part, represented business folks and land-owners who came for opportunity in the "New World". They looked with suspicion at the Indian folks and the Indian folks were suspicious as well. These immigrants knew nothing about raising crops and their hunting skills proved to be unproductive, as their only experience with hunting was "for sport". The first winter they nearly starved to death, so the Indians showed their spiritual goodness and educated them in all these things. So, in early America, the power*ful* listened to the power*less* and learned how to live!

The Powerful Followed. With growth came arrogance of power and an influx of organized churches. Again, the power*ful* slowly ignored the truth and wisdom of our original Americans. Military raided their camps, murdered their people, and drove them to live on government-designated lands— most not fit for farming or hunting.

In grief for his people, a Great Chief spoke again of spirituality:

> *This land belongs to us, for the Great Spirit gave it to us when he put us here. We were free to come and go, and to live in our own way. But white men who belong to another land, have come upon us and are forcing us to live according to their ideas. That is an injustice; we have never dreamed of making white men live as we live.*
>
> *White men like to dig in the ground for food. My people prefer to hunt the buffalo as their fathers did. White men like to stay in one place. My people want to live in tipis here and there to the different hunting grounds. The life of white men is slavery. They are prisoners in towns and farms. The life my*

10

people want is a life of freedom. I have seen nothing that a white man has, houses or railways or clothing or food, that is as good as the right to move in the open country, and live in our own fashion. Why has our blood been shed by your soldiers? Tatanka Hotanka, Chief Sitting Bull, Lakota Chief. (Native Universe, page 192)

Chief Joseph of the Nez Perce stated it this way:

We were like deer. They were like grizzly bears . . . The Creative Power, when He made the Earth, made no marks, no lines of division or separation on it . . . the Earth was too sacred to be valued by or sold for silver or gold. (Native Universe, pg. 116)

Churches in America

Organized churches joined the government in setting up Indian Boarding Schools. These schools were located long distances from their parents. They were required to wear uniforms and cut their hair short; their native language was forbidden and discipline was very strict. The children suffered severe home sickness. The "Neo-Americanism" of our original Americans was begun and our government made every effort to destroy their spirituality but with little success, as many of the living elders refused to "let it go".

In *We Were Not The Savages,* Chief Joseph of the Nez-Perce tribe spoke of churches in this way:

> *We do not want churches because they will teach us to quarrel about God, as the Catholics and Protestants do. We do not want that. . . . We may quarrel with men about things on earth, but we never quarrel about the Great Spirit.*

> *I believe much trouble and blood would
> be saved if we opened our harts more. I
> will tell you in my way how the Indian sees
> things. The white man has more words to
> tell you how they look to him, but it does not
> require many words to seek the truth. . . .
> Too many misinterpretations have been
> made. . . Too many misunderstandings.*
>
> *The Great Spirit Chief who rules above all
> will smile upon this land. . And this time
> the Indian race is waiting and praying.*

Of course, at the time of Christ, there were tabernacles, synagogues and "temples"; but Christ came and defined a different kind of tabernacle, synagogue and temple:

> *When Christ came as high priest of the good
> things that are already here, he went through
> the greater and more perfect tabernacle, that
> is not man-made. . . . Don't you know that
> you yourselves are God's Temple and that
> God's spirit lives in you?* (Hebrews 9:11)

The Pledge of Allegiance adopted for our nation at the beginning, stated:

> *I pledge allegiance to the flag of the United
> States of America and to the republic for
> which it stands: One Nation, Indivisible,
> with liberty and justice for all.*

14

This Pledge served our people well through wars, depressions and times of peace with no statement regarding religion and as a result, our people were free to worship or not to worship. No one could prevent another from worship nor could anyone be forced to worship. Youth organizations were free to use school property for meetings so long as no child was forced to participate. We truly were a nation that supported liberty and justice for all, with no religious requirements. Separation of church and state was the law of the land.

Following WWII, in our humble thankfulness that the war had ended, some in government decided that we needed to honor God's blessings by changing our Pledge of Allegiance to . . .

> . . . . *One Nation **under God**, indivisible, with liberty and justice for all.*

That opened the door for dogmatic religious influence to enter politics. Prior to that, personal religious beliefs were left out of politics in favor of patriotic ideals.

So, what do we have today? Folks mumble those words with little awareness of what they are saying. Our government forbids a non-sectarian prayer to God at the start of the school day and privately-supported youth organizations that require belief in God can no longer use school property. Compassionate hugs are forbidden and result in many cases, to expulsion from school. There is little reverence for life; our justice system is wrought with injustice; our music is filled with degradation of women;

and entertainment no longer sells unless it contains lurid sex scenes.

Since we became a nation "Under God", we have produced a society in which our government today supports reckless behavior. There is an attitude that work at lower-skilled jobs is not honorable. Fault lies with both government and society. God expects all works to be equally honorable:

> *There are different kinds of gifts, but the same Spirit. There are different kinds of service, but the same Lord. There are different kinds of working, but the same God works all of them in all men.*
>
> *Now to each one, the manifestation of the Spirit is given for the common good. To one there is given through the Spirit the message of wisdom, to another the message of knowledge by means of the same Spirit, to another faith by the same Spirit, to another gifts of healing by that One Spirit. . . .*
> *All these are the works of one and the same Spirit and he gives them in each one, just as he determines. (The early missionary Paul to the Corinthians in I Cor: 12:6-11)*

Today, the healthy non-working consider themselves mere victims of society and the government supports this hopeless attitude with un-earned paychecks that result in lives wasted.

Our government today accepts responsibility for the destructive sexual behavior of our teenage mothers, while the fathers of those babies continue their destructive behavior. Where are the parents of these teenagers? No worry for them, the government is taking care of things.

God's freedom demands responsibility as stated by the Apostle Peter:

> *Live as free men, but do not use your freedom as a cover-up for evil. (I Pet 2:16)*

Then, the missionary Paul spoke of freedom in this way:

> *You, my brothers, were called to be free. But do not use your freedom to indulge in sinful nature; rather, serve one another in love. The entire law is summed up in a single command: 'Love your neighbor as yourself'. (Gal. 5:13-14)*

Now, a nation that pledges to be "under God' most certainly should meet God's needs for its people; however it should not support the consequences of destructive life-styles nor provide unearned financial support for healthy individuals.   Those needs are best addressed by the private sector, which has the potential to turn lives around. Have we forgotten that America was built upon a "can-do" society— people helping people, people encouraging people?

Born into the culture of Christianity, I am thankful for the teachings of Jesus Christ. In regards to what it means to be "One Nation Under God", I believe our government should encourage opportunity for all, self-determination that "lifts up" all who are willing to do their part, a people who behave with an attitude that truly reflects honor and respect for all, regardless of social or economic class.

The early Christian Missionary Paul expressed this so well in his Letter to the Phillippines, Chapter 2, Verses 3 & 4:

> *Do nothing out of selfish ambition or vain conceit, but in humility, consider others better than yourselves. Each of you should look not only to your own interests but also to the interests of others.*

Leading with that attitude will truly raise up our Nation as one of truth and integrity around the world.

Many powerful leaders today continue to ignore the wisdom of both rich and poor. They wear their halo of dogmatic religious extremism to justify a corrupt judicial system and the destruction of innocent people in other parts of the world, when they fail to listen or consider words of truth and wisdom spoken by others.

Spirituality in Another Part
of the World

Let's revisit the land where Christ, the "Prince of Peace" was born, lived, and died, known as Palestine. Christians, Muslims, and Jews respected one another and lived in peace.

When WWII ended in Europe, the centuries-old Palestinian population lived in total peace. "Love thy neighbor" was the law of the land for all the people. The Melkite Christians dated back to the first Century, the beginning of Christianity and in the book: *Blood Brothers*, the Melkite priest, Elias Chacour, describes how the news of an Israel state was presented to his father who, in turn, presented it to the family:

> *In Europe, there was a man called Hitler.*
> *. . For a long time, he was killing Jewish*
> *people. . .just because they were Jews. For*
> *no other reason.*

He went on to say,

> *Now, this Hitler is dead. . . But our Jewish brothers have been badly hurt and frightened. They can't go back to their homes in Europe and they have not been welcomed by the rest of the world. So, they are coming here to look for a home. In a few days, children, Jewish soldiers will be traveling through Biram. They are Zionists. A few will stay in each home. . . maybe a week. Then they will move on. They have machine guns, but they don't kill. . .We must be especially kind and make them feel at home.* (Blood Brothers, page 20)

However, it turned out, these good people of Palestine were lied to and rather than allowing them to accept the newcomers with a compassionate welcome to share their land, the wealthy, well-armed Zionists from Europe drove them from their homes, closed their schools and libraries and forced them to live "out in the cold". The United Nations, with no questions asked from the world of nations, awarded the Zionists 54% of the land in which 70-90% of the population was Palestinian. This included the most fertile land of huge citrus groves and the land of the Bedouins where most of the barley and grain was grown. In other words, the Palestinians were made to hand over more than half of the well-cultivated land that produced their only livelihood.

Still, not one nation in the Western world questioned the plight of the Palestinian people as it worsened under the extreme Zionist leadership of Menachem Begin, who proclaimed publicly his goal to "purify the land of Palestinian people". *(Blood Brothers*, pg 47)

It is stated that the native Jewish population was shocked and grieved to learn of entire Palestinian families found dead in their homes from machine gun fire and massive knifings. They protested that such activities violated their ancient beliefs, to no avail. They were power*less* to help. No one listened.

Of course, the Zionists were not the poor survivors of the holocaust, but rather the power-hungry Jews from Europe who grabbed the opportunity for personal gain. One can only wonder how a Jewish person could treat others as theirs were treated by Hitler?

The abuse by the Zionists opened the door for religious extremists from all cultures to get into the act. Taking advantage of the occupation to promote their extreme views to political leaders, they pushed voices of "truth and wisdom" aside. The tragedies that result when religious fervor becomes political instead of spiritual are obviously clear.

Through secret arrangements, Elias Chacour, was sent to Paris to study for the priesthood. Near the end of his studies, his dear friend, Faraj, lamented regarding the lack of Western interest in the fate of the Palestinian people:

> *People in the West seem so taken with material things. It's as if they have nothing*

> *in their spirits, so they need to surround themselves with nice comforts. . . I hate to say it, but that sort of thinking seems to have invaded the Church too. . . The real problem. . . is that Western theology starts with man as the center of all things and tries to force God into some scheme that we can understand. Then He can be regulated. Elias, we've grown up believing that God is the beginning and the end of all things. He is central, not an afterthought. He's alive and has His own ways. Here, they want to tame God with their philosophy. (Blood Brothers, pg 109)*

Then Elias responded:

> *Worse than that. . . I'm afraid the Western philosophies have killed God. If there's no respect for Him, what value do men have? Without God, there is no compassion, no humanity. (Blood Brothers, pp 109-110)*

Elias, of course, struggled to find a way to help his people when he returned to Palestine:

> *If I were merely railing against a political system, that would be one thing . . . then I would become a politician. . . But I believe it is more than that. It's a spiritual sickness. There are unholy alliances between nations that talk about God while their true motives*

are purely military. (Blood Brothers, Pg 128)

Father Longere, Elias' professor, offered the following in one of his final lectures:

> *If there is a problem somewhere. . . this is what happens. Three people will try to do something concrete to settle the issue. Ten people will give a lecture analyzing what the three are doing. One hundred people will commend or condemn the ten for their lecture. One thousand people will argue about the problem. And one person—only one—will involve himself so deeply in the true solution that he is too busy to listen to any of it. . . Now, which person are you? (Blood Brothers, pg. 129)*

Soon it became quite clear that Elias Chacour was indeed that One. His arrival to the port of Haifa was marked with the reality of the lives of his people. Upon showing his passport for entry, he was very coldly instructed to go to another room and of course when he questioned why, the answer was "You are Palestinian". He was harshly interrogated, treated as an enemy, despite his insistence that he was a returning seminary student. Following about 1-1/2 hours of such questioning, he was then told to "strip". That, he refused to do, telling them "This is my limit — I will not strip". Of course, they threatened to deny entry unless he complied; but he courageously stood by his decision, sat down, took out a book and began reading. The interrogator asked him what he was doing and he answered, "You are not going to admit me and I am not going to strip, so I am going to sit here and read a book". The stalemate ended after about eight very nerve-wracking hours and he was finally admitted to his country.

Father Elias Chacour was deeply saddened by all he heard and all he saw of the violence that had resulted as youths were forced to live hopeless lives, a result of the military crackdown against the Palestinians. As he waited for his first assignment from the Bishop, his nights were restless with images of bright but aimless young men, their lives wasting without opportunity; of grenades exploding and both Palestinian and Jewish children being ripped apart.

He decided to return to his home village of Biram, as he had learned the soldiers had abandoned it. He arrived to find a village of ruined stone houses and a shell of the church. But something spiritual was at work for, as he stood in silent awe of the wreckage of his village, his home and his childhood church, he began to focus on the message of Jesus, how he took up for the weak, the outcasts, etc.— that one of the first things Jesus did to reconcile man to God was to restore human dignity in all. Then, his thoughts returned to the Beatitudes that were deeply ingrained throughout his childhood by his mother.

When his assignment from the Bishop came, it was to serve the very tiny, very poor village of Ibillin. He found a population that had simply "gone along" in order to survive and were very suspicious of a newcomer, even a Priest. He was greeted with nothing but hostility. However, despite that welcome, his commitment to peace and justice prevailed and he never gave up on his spiritual purpose.

Today, as pastor of St. Jospeh Church in Ibillin, which is near the Golan Heights, he has established the village as one of nonviolence and interfaith understanding. Beginning in the early 1980s, he launched an educational project that began with 20 students and grew today to become known as the Mar Elias Educational Institutions, serving more than 4,000 students from kindergarten to college regardless of religious affiliation, made possible by private contributions from peace-loving folks of all religious cultures. He lives his belief that human dignity and education are the road to peace among peoples as they are able to move beyond poverty and the violence it generates.

However, due to the lack of attention to his success by the Power*ful* in the political world and the mainstream news media, the root of the violence in Palestine continues to be misunderstood.

Upon publication of his book, *Blood Brothers*, Elias Chacour toured America in hopes of gaining understanding and support for the Palestinian cause. However, the power of the Zionist influence in America was too deeply ingrained in the minds of our people and politicians. Zionist propaganda had already convinced Americans that the Jews were the sole victims and American money interests poured in for their defense. Thanks to America's failure to listen to the voices of the power*less*, the Israeli military is second only to that of the United States. It is puzzling how our government, "Under God', failed to recognize the take-over and abuse of what was once a very peaceful part of our world, folks ready to welcome the victims of the holocaust with open arms.

This takes me to the question of "who" or "what" killed Jesus Christ. Christ was no politician but rather, I believe, was sent by God to teach us how God expects us to live. However, political jealousy took his life and I cannot but wonder if today, as some "use" his name to gain political favor, are they not killing his message of love? Father Elias Chacour is a hero of the Power*less* who speak truth and wisdom to spread the message of love to all and in spite of the fact that the Power*ful* fail to listen, he continues on his journey for peace in the part of the world where he finds opportunity to meet God's needs for all people without prejudice towards religious culture.

He has reached thousands through his writings in *Blood Brothers* and *We Belong to the Land*. His message to his readers is:

> *If you have been enlightened enough to take the side of the Palestinians—oh bless your hearts—take our sides, because for once you will be on the right side, right? But if taking our side would mean to become one-sided against my Jewish brothers and sisters, backup. We do not need such friendship.*

*We need one more common friend. We do
not need one more enemy, for God's sake.*
(Profiles of Peace)

He has worked tirelessly promoting nonviolent change in
Israeli society and for his efforts, he has been nominated
several times for the Nobel Peace Prize. But does
mainstream America know this?

The Millennium, January 1, 2000

At the end of the year 1999, Charles Sennott of the *Boston Globe* traveled to the Holy Land to report on conditions of the Palestinian Christians. Of course, by that time, their lives were under great duress from decades of abuse at the hands of the powerful Zionist military.

In the land where Christ lived and died, Mr. Sennott walked where Jesus had walked, visited with folks of many different faiths and observed activities leading up to midnight, December 31, 1999. His first-hand reports resulted in publication of his book: *The Body and the Blood*. After reading this book, it is difficult to reason why some who consider themselves Christian continue to support the work of the Zionists with no sympathy or understanding of the plight of the original inhabitants of Palestine--Christians, Muslims, and Jews. Like the tragedies imposed upon our American Indians, one can only ask: have we learned nothing?

Mr. Sennott's interviews revealed tremendous sadness and tragedies that none in our country can possibly imagine. An example is this interview with Mr. Shafiq

Elias Bisharat, born in Palestine in 1925. He was sitting in the shade of a pine tree, resting before the long walk to his old village, a walk he had taken yearly. Mr. Sennott offered to drive him and he accepted. On the way, they passed a Muslim cemetery, where weeds had grown up over the tombstones. He had them stop to recall a few family names that could barely be read as the granites were cracked and broken. He stated:

> *We were one soul. . . At weddings it was*
> *traditional to have not one best man but*
> *two – a Muslim and a Christian. (Body*
> *and the Blood, pg. 90)*

Now, the cemetery was surrounded by barbed wire to divide it from an Israeli military site to protect a nearby airport. The Christian cemetery could be seen barely as one peered through the barbed wire and ten-foot-high crates filled with ammunition. Shaffiq stated that most of his ancestors are buried there, but he had not been allowed to visit their graves for over 52 years.

They arrived at the old village to find the remains of a mosque, mostly destroyed, and the Christian Melkite church, mostly destroyed. Shafiq stated, sadly:

> *In all my dreams, I see myself back in this*
> *town. It was a life that you cannot imagine,*
> *a time of absolute happiness. (Body and the*
> *Blood, pg 90)*

Continuing on, where homes once stood were now collapsed mounds of hand-hewn stones piled in an overgrown field. Shafiq led Mr. Sennott to a crumbled circular foundation just off to the side of what once was his home. He removed a wooden cover to expose a 20-foot-deep well, stating:

> *I dug this well with my own hands. It took*
> *me two years, and I had just finished when*
> *the war broke out. (Body and the Blood,*
> *pg. 91)*

Sadly, this story was repeated over and over again, all because of the collective guilt of the Western World over the Holocaust in which the Palestinian people had played no part.

The 1967 War found many young Palestinians studying abroad with the intent to return to their home land as educated professionals. However, while they were away, the Zionists conducted a census of all non-Jewish residents and those studying away were left out of the census. When they attempted to return, they were denied entrance to their own country. Charles Sennott interviewed one such couple, Alma and Kamal Hazboun. Their beautiful old home in Bethlehem now stands empty, windows broken out. Two children have been born to them in the United States and he had a highly respected job with an American corporation.

Alma and Kamal and their children were in the country for the Christmas Holiday, on a tourist visa. His frustrations with the plight of his people were expressed this way:

> *I have a U.S. passport. My children were born in America. I pay taxes. I have voted in five Presidential elections in America. But I can't return to my homeland. Even though I have a birth certificate from the Church of the Nativity in Bethlehem, even though my parents' house sits vacant, even though we can trace our lineage back hundreds of years, none of this is considered proof of citizenship by the Israelis.*

He continued:

> *But, if you are from New York or Moscow and you are born Jewish, you have the right to become a citizen in Israel the minute you land at the airport. Do you know what that does to you? (The Body and the Blood, pg. 17)*

Kamal was referring to the Israeli law of return, which permits anyone with a Jewish grandparent to live in Israel with a guarantee of financial assistance as they make the move. He continued the conversation:

> *It is very difficult trying to make Americans, our neighbors and friends, our colleagues at work, our fellow parishioners at church, comprehend these facts. Even the very*

> *educated in America just have no idea what*
> *is going on here, or the injustices that take*
> *place. (The Body and the Blood, pg. 18)*

His wife, Alma, added:

> *When you live in America, you learn what*
> *freedom means. . . and I think it makes it*
> *impossible to ever think of coming back to*
> *this, to the checkpoints, and the humiliation,*
> *and the daily outrages of life here. I miss*
> *it. This is my home. But we cannot come*
> *home. (The Body and the Blood, pg 18)*

Kamal speaks of the humiliation his family suffered as they traveled to visit Bethlehem at this Christmas Time. On their way, they and the children were taken aside; their bags taken to a back room where they were emptied out. They were asked to wait to one side of the line, while dozens of other passengers went ahead of them. Finally, they were let through. Kamal expressed his anger to Mr. Sennott:

> *All I can think, standing in line, is that*
> *I am an American taxpayer, contributing*
> *to the billions of dollars in taxes that go to*
> *Israel. . . I get furious knowing what life is*
> *like for our families and friends back home,*
> *knowing how brutal this occupation was,*
> *and knowing that all these forces of history*
> *and economics were pushing our people,*
> *including Christians, off of this land, even*

> *right here where Jesus was born. (The Body*
> *and the Blood, pg. 18)*

Even more revealing of how Christians in America have lost their way is Sennott's description of organized activities in the Holy Land on December 31, 1999. Many extreme Evangelical Christians believed that the "Second Coming" would occur at that time and had gathered to celebrate, believing they would be favored while all others would be left behind. One group of several hundred gathered at the Garden Tomb for a raucous night of singing and prayers to usher in the New Year. Following the service, as they enjoyed cookies and coffee, the pastor stated that it seemed the reporters were upset that nothing happened, that the only people talking about the new year as the time of return of the Messiah were the TV and newspaper reporters. Was he trying to appear innocent in all of that madness? Yes, the world did not come to an end and next morning folks went about business as usual. The evangelicals came to celebrate something of their own imaginations and returned to America, still ignorant of the plight of the true Christians, born in the land where Jesus lived and died and they continue to support the misled Zionist movement.

Charles Sennott's visit with Mayor Jeraisi of Nazareth is especially interesting. The Mayor, son of an Orthodox Priest, stated that his family celebrates the feasts of Christmas and Easter, but that they stop there. He stated that he grew up never knowing whether friends and neighbors were Muslim or Christian, that no one asked and no one cared; that in his view of the past, everyone got along. Regarding his faith, he stated:

> *I believe there is a God. I believe all of the*
> *prophets were revolutionaries in their time*
> *who tried to bring people to human values.*
> *But the followers of religion, when they*
> *bring politics into their religion, have gone*
> *down a dangerous path. Religion is based*
> *on emotions and beliefs and it has great*
> *force to influence people and to appeal to the*
> *weakness of people and it is very dangerous.*
> *(The Body and the Blood, p. 21*

The Refugees

Thousands of Palestinian refugees, Christian and Muslim, poured across the borders to neighboring countries. The Kingdom of Jordan made room for most by numbers.

People of wisdom and goodness are found among all cultures, all nationalities, all religions. Regarding the Palestinian tragedies, examples of the tireless efforts of the late King Hussein of Jordan and his beautiful American-born wife, Lisa Halaby, who became Queen Noor of Jordan, are beautifully and sadly described in her book, *Leap of Faith*.

Queen Noor provides a unique inside story of their combined efforts to bring peace and hope to the region and their genuine love for all humanity. However, just as it was here in early America, such efforts by the power*less* fell by the wayside, ambushed by broken promises and greed. When the helpless Palestinians attempted to protect their land and their lives from the well-armed Israeli military, they were tagged as terrorists and received little sympathy from those in the U.S. Congress. Queen Noor was very troubled by this; however, it should not have been a surprise, for here in America, the Israeli lobby is well-funded by wealthy Jewish bankers and business leaders who throw their financial support to elected officials who agree to bow to their Zionist activities.

At the time of her marriage, Queen Noor was not active in organized religion. She states in her book that her father encouraged her to find her own path to spirituality. Her marriage to the King did not require that she join the Islam faith. However, over time, she gained much admiration for its teachings, which she describes:

> *I admired Islam's emphasis on a believer's direct relationship with God, the fundamental equality of rights of all men and women, and the reverence for the Prophet Muhammad as well as all the Prophets and messengers who came before him, since Adam, to Abraham, Moses, Jesus, and many others. Islam calls for fairness, tolerance, and charity. 'Let there be no compulsion in religion' the Quran commands and 'Not one of you is a true believer until he desires for his brother what he desires for himself'. . . . I was attracted too, by its simplicity and call for justice. Islam is a very personal belief system. There are prayer leaders and religious scholars but no intermediaries or bureaucrats, as in other monotheistic religions. . . Honesty, faithfulness and moderation are a few of the virtues that Islam calls for . . (Leap of Faith, pg 96)*

Their life-style was very conservative compared to that of leaders of other Kingdoms. There were no ornate castles but rather homes filled with the laughter of many children and lots of pets of many varieties. Over the years of the Zionist occupation, thousands of poor Palestinian refugees who had lost their homes poured into Jordan and placed immense financial strain on the Jordanian country to meet the simple basic needs of so many who arrived with nothing. Queen Noor described the goodness of her husband in this way:

> *Hussein personally supported the expenses of our home and of the extended royal family through financial resources he was given from within the Arab and Muslim world. He had a basic allowance from the government that had not changed in all his years as King, and neither of us took any personal money from the Jordanian government. In a crunch, he would sell his assets in order to cover Royal Court bills, which were largely devoted to health and education assistance or to support institutions in need. . . . He believed that if he was a faithful Muslim who focused more on the needs of others than on his own, God would enable him to continue his good works. This was not an MBA's approach to finance, but it could not have been. It was an ethical and humane balance that Hussein struck within the context of an environment that did not*

> *function like the West, that was constantly fluid and uncertain and sometimes prone to extremes. The King would never turn away from someone in need. Many a morning he would listen to a local call-in show called 'Live Transmissions' and be stirred to offer assistance to someone in dire circumstances. At times his generosity seemed arbitrary, but like a traditional tribal leader, he often used it to maintain a complex political balance. In any event, the money went out as fast as it came in and somehow it all worked out. (Leap of Faith, pp 225-226)*

In recalling the sadness of her husband's death and his tireless efforts for peace, she shared the following, a clearly stated purpose:

> *Life and death—both are stages in the journey of the spirit, both are entirely in God's hands. Hussein often said that we are mere custodians of a timeless legacy that transcends any single person, country, or culture. We are momentary and mortal bearers of eternal, sacred values that have been handed down generation after generation—in our region and elsewhere for thousands of years. . . .for change to be positive and lasting, we must all acknowledge our common humanity and live by the shared values of our faiths. . . 'Not one of you is a true believer until he desires for his brother what he desires for himself'. (Leap of Faith, pg 439)*

The final words in her book are to her husband's memory:

> *I know that Hussein's achievements will endure long in history, but it will be the memory of his loving eyes and smile, gentle humor and confident wisdom, his humble, generous and forgiving spirit that will enable me to go on. I pray that his legacy of love, tolerance, and peace lives on in all of us—it is his gift and challenge for which I will be eternally grateful and will seek to uphold in my life and work*

Queen Noor then pens a dear message to her husband, the King::

> *I will not fail you, my love, I will continue on the path we shared, and I know you will be there to help me, as you always were. And when we meet again at the journey's end, and we laugh together once more, I will have a thousand things to tell you.*

> *Noor Al Hussein*
> *Bab al Salem*
> *Amman, Jordan, November 2002*
> *Ramadan 1423*

(Leap of Faith, pp. 439-440)

Shamefully, here in America, some are much like the quarreling family of children, God's children, each claiming favoritism and some resorting to extreme measures to gain public support for views that are more cultural than spiritual, ignoring the important American Beliefs as stated in our Pledge of Allegiance:

> " I pledge allegiance to the flag of the United States of America and the republic for which it stands, One Nation Under God, indivisible, with Liberty and Justice for all."

Dogmatic Beliefs Harm America

The Zionists use their dogmatic beliefs against all who
disagree with them, even their Jewish brothers who live
their laws as stated by Moses in the Old Testament Book
of Leviticus, Chapter 19:

> *Do not defraud your neighbor or rob him.*
> *Do not hold back the wages of a hired man*
>   *overnight.*
> *Do not pervert justice; do not show partiality*
>   *to the poor or favoritism to the great,*
>   *but judge your neighbor fairly.*
> *Do not go about spreading slander among*
>   *your people.*
> *Do not do anything that endangers your*
>   *neighbor's life.*
> *Do not hate your brother in your heart. . .*
>   *do not seek revenge. . . but love your*
>   *neighbor as yourself.*

And then in Chapter 25:

> *The land is mine and you are but aliens And*
> *tenants (thus sayeth the Lord).*

So, my dear Readers, considering the treatment of the peaceful folks who lovingly cared for the land of the Palestinians before Zionist control, do you not see that the Zionists are either ignorant of Jewish Laws or simply prefer to ignore them in pursuit of power and control over others?

Now, let's look at the Evangelicals who have joined the Zionists in their quest for power and control. The word "Evangelical" when used with the word "Movement" depicts a political rather than spiritual connotation. The "Movement" is one that thrives on religious fear rather than love, that they alone will be separated from the rest at the "Second Coming of Christ", raised to paradise leaving everyone else behind to live in total destruction. Is that the message of Christ? They meet in huge arenas, which they own, and the services are more entertainment-centered than spiritual and some even resemble political conventions with loud and raucous enthusiasm for the on-stage entertainer. I call their attention to II Timothy 4:3:

> *For the time will come when men will not put up with sound doctrine. Instead, to suit their own desires, they will gather around them a great number of teachers to say what their itching ears want to hear.*

While mainstream Evangelical Christians are committed to and live by their own interpretation of religion, the "Movement" is a political organization that financially supports the "Zionist Movement" in hopes the Zionists will further their cause.

The "Movement" would like for the world to view them as devout Christians; however, Christ was sent by God to deliver a New Covenant, the New Testament, which simplifies all laws under that one great commandment: *to love the Lord your God with all your heart, all your mind, all your soul, and your neighbor as yourself.*

Christ emphasized that this one commandment takes the place of all other laws, thus allowing us to follow the teachings of Christ without the complexity of the past, simply to have God in our daily lives, love him and our neighbors without prejudice, and above all never to judge the faith or spirituality of others.

All other Believers, who greatly outnumber those in the "Movement", enter their cathedrals, synagogues, mosques, small churches and the immensity of the Great Outdoors and stand in awe of the spiritual presence of God, which is so sweetly described in the following hymn:

> *Surely, the presence of God is in this place*
> *I can feel his mighty power and his grace,*
> *I can hear the brush of angels' wings*
> *I see glory on each face.*
> *Surely, the presence of God is in this place.*

Be Still and Know I Am God

As Americans, our leaders must honor the goodness of all peoples on this earth, regardless of the avenue through which they reach God. They must recognize that it is God who unites us all, irrespective of differences in cultures or life-style. My writings are, in no way, meant to discount the good done by people of organized religion; but rather to point out that they are good only when they encourage their members to meet God's needs for people with the sole purpose of doing good without obligation. It's all about purpose, what is in the heart!

While the Zionists and Evangelicals are committed mostly to raising large sums of money to win political favor, the devout, true Believers continue, in their humble ways, to do God's goodness for all people, within their personal means and from their hearts. Those who do good for others, regardless of culture or religion are truly pleasing God .

In Luke 32:33, Christ admonishes the rest:

> *If you love those who love you, what credit is that to you? Even sinners love those who love them. And if you do good to those who are good to you, what credit is that to you? Even sinners do that.*

Yes, it is America's tragedy that the spirituality of our forefathers suffers from the slow and gradual infiltration of the single-minded Zionists-Evangelical movement into our judicial and governmental affairs. Flag pins and crosses have been promoted as symbols of a particular political party.   In grief for my country, my beautiful cross is safely tucked away in my jewelry box, waiting for the day that our country is once again led by truly patriotic citizens who, when they enter to govern, leave their personal cultural beliefs at the door with total commitment to all Americans through obedience to our Pledge of Allegiance, "One Nation Under God, Indivisible, with liberty and justice for all"--then, and only then, will I wear that beautiful cross, for the meaning will no longer be tarnished by politics.

A New Gospel

The Holy Bible is a collection of religious history and personal accounts of the Life of Jesus, recorded by folks who lived during the time of Christ and early missionaries that followed. The book of John is considered a very important and beloved record of the life and teachings of Jesus Christ. The final verse Chapter 21, states that:

> *Jesus did many other things as well. If every one of them were written down, I suppose that even the whole world would not have room for all the books that would be written.*

One such recorded story regarding the messages of Jesus, was recently discovered in archeological diggings in Egypt. A review of the translations were made available by Elaine Pagels in her book, *The Secret Gospel of Thomas.*

The story of Thomas as recorded in the Bible leads us to believe that his faith was not as strong as the rest. However, intelligence requires that questions be asked and turns out, Thomas asked Christ many questions that one might believe took great courage. Both the questions and the answers were more direct and clear than recorded by others. The story of Thomas was among many not included in the Bible but was valued enough to be hidden safely in a jar, and buried for safe-keeping. With the world in the state it is in, one must surely believe, that God intended it to be discovered at this time.

So what does the Gospel of Thomas say — what is the Secret?

While much is "hinted at" in other Gospels, there is one very clear message that is new. Christ told Thomas that he came as God's son to bring "Light" into the world, and that the same Light is within all, that we too are children of God through the gift of His Image within each of us, our eternal soul; thus we need no one to intervene for us, that God is open to all who acknowledge Him through personal prayer..

Thomas asked several other questions, the answer more clearly stated to him:

How can we know ourselves?

Christ answered:

> *Find out first where you came from and go back and take your place in the Beginning. . . Blessed is the One who came into Being before he came into Being. (Beyond Belief, page 55)*

This challenges each of us to know our ancestors, seek to learn the goodness of their lives, learn from that, and then we will understand ourselves more completely.

Then Thomas asked Christ:

> *How should we live?*

Christ then answered:

> *The Kingdom is inside of you and outside of you. When you come to know yourselves then you will be known and you will see that it is you who are the children of the living Father. But if you will not know yourselves, you dwell in poverty and it is you who are that poverty. (Beyond Belief, p. 54)*

Then Christ continued:

> *If you bring forth what is within you, what you bring forth will save you. (Beyond Belief, p. 53)*

In other words, life on earth is an important continuation of the lives that went before and our ancestry is extremely important to our own well-being.

Next, Thomas asked a question we all ponder from time to time:

> *When will the end times come?*

Christ then answered:

> *What you look forward to has already come,*
> *but you do not recognize it. It will not come*
> *by waiting for it. It will not be a matter of*
> *saying, 'Here it is or 'There it is'. Rather, the*
> *Kingdom of the Father is spread out upon*
> *the earth and people do not see it. (Beyond*
> *Belief, page 50)*

I believe that Heaven is right here on earth through the good feelings that come from doing for others, small deeds, words of encouragement, a friendly smile or pat on the back.

Then, in final summary, Christ said to Thomas:

> *Joy to those who receive from the Father the*
> *grace of knowing him. . . those who receive*
> *this Gospel no longer think of God as petty,*
> *nor harsh, nor wrathful. . . but as a Being*
> *without evil, loving, full of tranquility*
> *gracious and all knowing. (Beyond Belief,*
> *page 121)*

> *Human existence apart from God is a*
> *Nightmare but by discovering God's presence*
> *here and now, the terror lessens as his spirit*
> *extends a hand, lifts us up, supports us in all*
> *things and finally restores the soul. (Beyond*
> *Belief, page 120)*

So, again, Christ came to let the world know that there was a new law, a New Covenant, that God is full of love, compassion, and strength and that there is no place for fear in those who love him.

The Gospel of Thomas supports the spirituality I have known since the death of my parents. Both died young my father the last, from illness that lasted three years and, as with all who suffer from cancer, the final year was filled with pain and sadness. I knew he was ready to go and as I sat by his bedside the day before his death, I prayed silently that God listen to his prayers and mine; that we both wanted the suffering to end. As I sat in his room very early next morning, I suddenly realized that he was no longer there — his body, breathing with assistance. Then I became aware that Christ had entered the room and taken him away. It is my firm belief that the"Second Coming" occurs when Christ appears at our death to return us to the loving arms of God., proof found in the writings of the *Secret Gospel of Thomas.*

In 1991, I felt the need for my children to know my parents. So, I decided to research my family's history and also that of my husband's family. I decided to approach it all from the view of their religious beliefs and how those beliefs affected the way they lived. It was tremendously rewarding! However, in order to get started, I felt the need to develop my own philosophy as a base for beginning. So, the philosophy I recorded was this:

> *Threads. . . that make up the very fabric of our Being; the strengths handed down from generation to generation that give purpose to those who follow. These threads, carefully selected by our Maker, are of varied hues to give us balance of beauty and purpose. Families have obligations known only to God and the threads continued throughout generations are those important to His Kingdom on Earth as well as in Heaven. You may never know greatness during your lifetime, but your contributions are important to His Plan. To find true happiness in this life, we must alert ourselves to these strengths and obligations–accept them as true gifts, be forever thankful for them, and never let ourselves forget that our talents, our abilities, and everything we own belong to God–that He has entrusted them to us to be used wisely and without greed. . . Be alert and proud. Pursue your life with faith and confidence, and despite a few flaws, your Threads will become part of an original masterpiece of God's work through which others will come to know Him.*

Written about 15 years before I knew of the *Secret Gospel of Thomas,* I was surprised how much my words mirrored those in that Gospel. Then today, as I read the religious philosophy of my Indian friends, I find that my words are much like theirs and wonder if perhaps they were planted in me at my birth through that beautiful gift of beads!

My four books: Tillerson, Patty P.: *Threads, Books I, II, III, and IV,* are available in many geneology libraries around the country.

The New Gospel and the Spirituality of Ancient People

From the stories handed down from the ancient ones, it is clear that they most surely knew God and revered Him through their ceremonies and their way of life. These stories have been nicely recorded in the beautiful book: *Native Universe: Voices of Indian America.*

Comparing some of those writings to those of the New Gospel of Thomas, here is a quote found on page 16:

Native people believe that unseen powers and creative forces formed the Earth, sun, stars, moon, mountains, oceans, rivers, lakes, valleys, plains, and other elements of the natural environment. The Creator made the Native Universe in a variety of ways with forethought and knowledge, not in a haphazard manner. Emergence came with spirit, imagination, and design, and humans are only one small portion of the creation, a part of the universal whole that remains a great mystery.

The writing goes on to state that creative forces set the world in motion and that those same creative forces exist today in the work of Native American poets, artists, dancers, and singers.

Continuing:

> *These spirits are alive in every cell, every atom of the Native Universe. They are a part of the whole, the agent that brought forth and keeps life in motion.*

Does this not agree with the Gospel of Thomas when Christ told him to "bring forth what is within you"?

Regarding the meaning of ceremonies, John C. Mohawk describes them in this way:

> *Health, well-being, and honor are much a part of . . . ceremonies, not just for participants but for people throughout the world. The Hupa pray and sing for others, as they pray for themselves. . . Ceremonies provide the means for people to give thanks, ask for help, and renew their relationship with the temporal and spiritual worlds around them. (Page 47, Native Universe)*

Among the history provided in this remarkable book, page 36, is the importance of ancestry to the Indian people:

*Many native people believe that our dead
ancestors continue to influence our lives.
Saying that our relatives surround and
help us, elders teach us to remember and
honor the dead through good thoughts and
prayers.*

These are but brief statements from the historical records in *Native Universe*; however, this affirms my belief that those people did not need outside influences to teach them about God, for they knew him from the Beginning.

It is heart-breaking to know how these beautiful people were treated by immigrants who used power and military force to take away their lands, attempt to destroy their culture and their language and make them become "just like us".

There has been no greater hero for peace than Nez Perce Chief Joseph, whose tribe lived in peace with the white people through their friendship with Lewis and Clark. An early treaty allowed them to remain on most of their lands; however, that treaty, like all others, was broken and his people were sent to a reservation in Oklahoma where many died from disease and starvation. It is recorded that he died of a broken heart, but thankfully, his words of wisdom have survived. Consider these quotes recorded in *We Were Not The Savages:*

*Our fathers gave us many laws, which they
had learned from their fathers. These laws
were good. They told us to treat all people*

> *as they treated us; that we should never be the first to break a bargain; that it was a disgrace to tell a lie; that we should speak only the truth.*
>
> *Good words do not last long unless they amount to something. . . . I am tired of talk that comes to nothing It makes my heart sick when I remember all the good words and all the broken promises. There has been too much talking by men who had no right to talk.*
>
> *If the white man wants to live in peace with the Indian, he can live in peace. Treat all men alike. Give them a chance to live and grow.*
>
> *I am not a child, I think for myself. No man can think for me.*

Yes, and no National Leader has the right to define God for others–belief in God requires freedom of thought!

Among my treasures are the dolls pictured on the following pages.

All of these were purchased for me by my parents during two trips to New Mexico in the 1930s. The earrings pictured with the second picture were my first ones, at age 12 and I still wear them on occasion. I understand that dolls were a way for mothers to teach little girls about values, much like my mother taught me.

The first picture is a hand-made doll from corn husks. I understand that these were the first dolls made for little girls and were not expected to last.

The second picture is a hand-made doll, dressed in traditional clothing. Notice the details, the beads. It was traditional that the hair be from the mother's own hair—a very spiritual touch!

The third picture is a hand-carved Kachina, I am not sure, but I think it may be a religious priest?

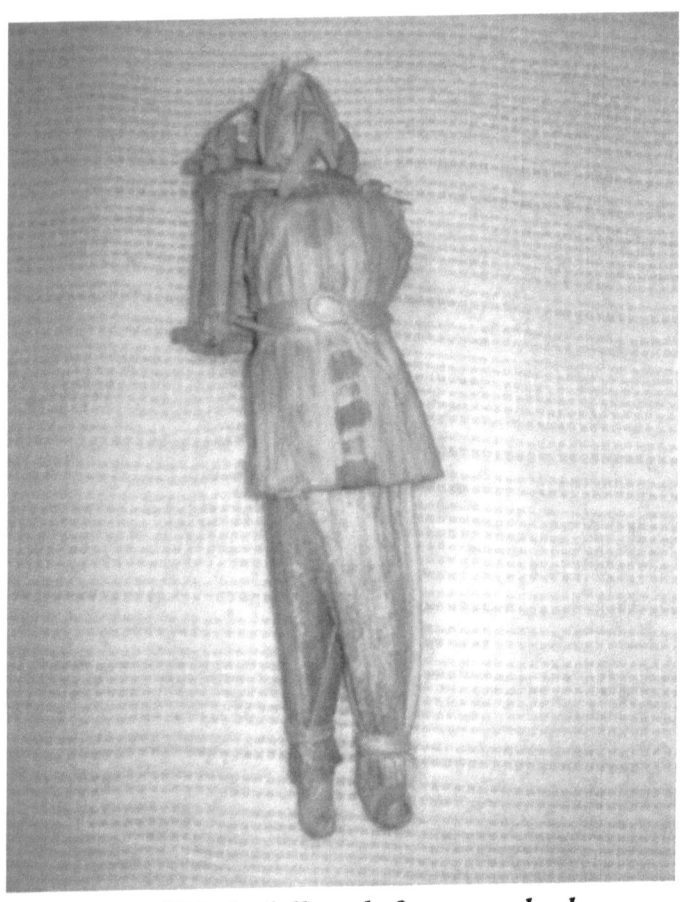

Hand-Made doll made from corn husks

Hand-made doll in traditional clothing

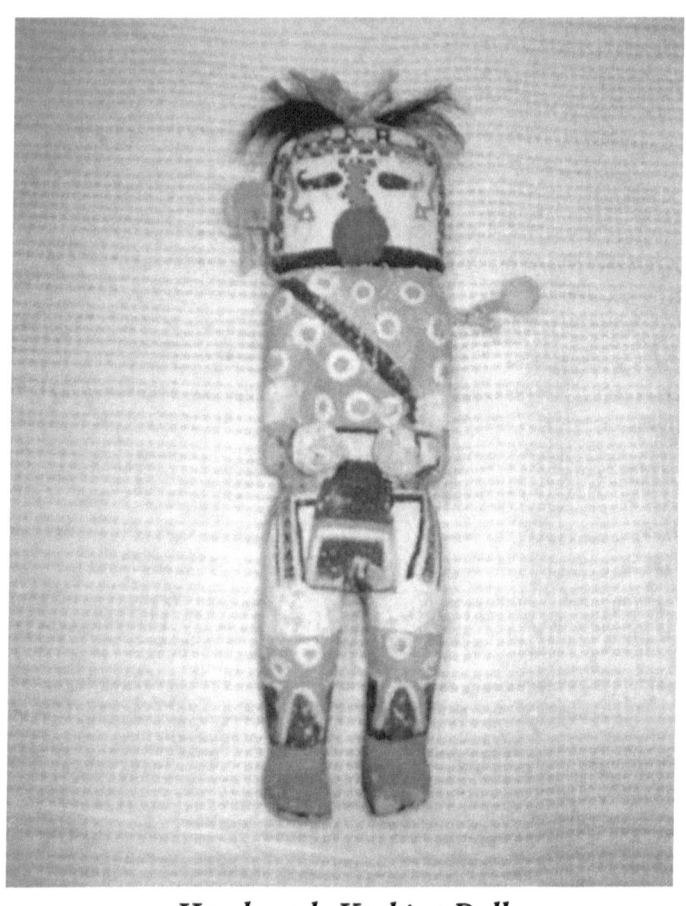

Hand-made Kachina Doll

Wise Folks, Great Accomplishments

While history is filled with broken treaties, fraudulent land deals and our government's efforts to destroy their culture and their language, descendants of our original Americans, our Indian friends, never lost their love for this land. Every time there have been threats to its security, they volunteered along with all other Americans to save this land from harm. They have been represented in large numbers in all branches of the armed services, in all wars, from the American Revolution through both World Wars and even to the present-day struggles.

Following the attack on Pearl Harbor, December 7, 1941, it is recorded that many showed up to volunteer carrying with them, their personal guns, knives, and even pitchforks to do their part!

Those unable to join the military worked alongside other Americans on the home front to support the war effort. Their people fought and died for this country through every war.

Especially noteworthy to victory in the Pacific were the Navajo Code Talkers, who created a secret code for communication based on their native language that was never broken by the Japanese. Without the code-talkers, many more American lives would have been lost on those Pacific Islands.

Today, their descendants are found in every walk of life, in all professions. Of course their art and jewelry are well-known but what is not so well-known is that their talents are found in the film industry and software design; as geologists and engineers; as professors and researchers, doctors and lawyers. Especially outstanding is the fact that in 2002, Chickasaw astronaut, John Herrington, carried with him as he orbited the earth, a Hopi ceramic pot made by his Hopi friend, Al Qoyawayma, a mechanical engineer who developed and patented internal guidance systems.

Cultural wisdom and spirituality is a common thread that lives in all to this day. Navajo Lori Arviso Alvord, M.D., expresses it in this way:

> *The Navajo belief system sees sickness as falling out of balance, of losing one's way on the path of beauty. The body must live in harmony with the Spirit. (Native Universe, pg. 243)*

Despite economic gains of a few, their voices for justice for all continue to go unheeded. A three-part investigative series in the *Denver Post*, November 11-13, 2007, uncovered just how troubling and tragic is the issue of justice on our Indian Reservations. The article described something that most of America doesn't understand about the legal system on Indian Reservations, how it is set up. While reservations employ their own policemen, prosecution for serious crimes is the sole authority of U.S. Attorneys, who are political appointees and serve at the discretion of the U.S. Attorney General.

Proof of how our government continues to pay little attention to the prosecution of serious crimes on reservations is revealed in this report: " that the Head of the Native American Issues Subcommittee was "denied a part as a key player in the Justice Department's *Attorney General Advisory Council,* while every other Head of a subcommittee was included".

Today, as a result of this neglectful attitude, murderers, rapists, etc. go free after a few days in the reservation jail. Janelle Doughty,   Head of Justice and Regulatory Affairs for the Southern Ute tribe in Colorado, stated the situation this way:

> *It's like, you've taken our land, You've taken our water. How can we trust that you'll take this case and take these people dear to our hearts and really take care of them? (Denver Post, November 13, 2007)*

Again, our government today ignores our pledge of **"Liberty and Justice for all",** while those in positions of power cater to their favored constituents and the power*less* cry for equality.

Hope and Honor

Despite the slow progress towards liberty and justice for our Indian friends, there is hope and honor for them today through the magnificent National Museum of the American Indian which is included in the National Smithsonian in Washington, D.C. This museum is unlike any other — its architectural design is focused upon the spirituality of the people and upon entering, one simply has the desire to stand back in awe and "drink in the beauty".

Finally, our original Americans are able to show-case the truth of who they are, their reverence for all of God's creatures. One example of this was in the dresses they made, described here by Keri Jhane Myers, Comanche, 2005:

> *We try to use everything in its natural form. When you folded a deer-hide over to make the top for a three-hide dress, two legs would hang on each side of the dress. They were kept as a marker to show that we still respected the animals that the hides came from.*

The displays of dresses, the ornate beadings, and the stories surrounding them speak of the awesome spirituality of the people. The importance of this museum is briefly stated by Jackie Parsons of the Blackfeet tribe, 2005:

> *It's important to preserve the culture. There are three things that maintain a culture – language, religion, and art. You lose those three, and you lose the culture completely. So it's very important to retain all of them.*

Regarding lackluster efforts of the past to exhibit what our Indian friends stood for, is this quote by Paul Chaat Smith, Comanche, from *Native Voices, p.184:*

> *I ponder these questions now from the vantage of the Smithsonian National Museum of the American Indian, with its centerpiece building situated on what was the last open space on the National Mall. This might be the most amazing piece of earth in America. From above, the Mall is like a jigsaw puzzle. There is Washington, the father of the country, and Lincoln who saved it. A great art museum to rival any in Europe on one side, a vast warehouse of the American rockets that conquered space on the other. It is America at its best, a country big enough and generous enough to not only acknowledge a fiasco like Vietnam but to remember it with the stunning black*

*granite walls of the Vietnam Memorial.
African slave labor built the Capitol Dome
yet it signals freedom and hope in spite of
that, or perhaps because of it. The Mall is a
fabulously weird theme park of the country's
idea of itself over the last few centuries, a
boulevard of broken dreams, liberation,
and astonishing achievement. The planet's
smart money is still betting Lincoln was
right, that this is Man's last best hope and is
there greater proof of America's outrageous
ability to change (and not change) than this
new palace carved from Indian rock and
dedicated to the preposterous, wonderful,
and breathtakingly ambitious task of telling
the stories of Native peoples from throughout
the hemisphere and throughout time?*

So, let's review Lincoln's immortal "Gettysburg
Address":

*Four score and seven years ago, our fathers
brought forth upon this continent a new
nation: conceived in liberty, and dedicated
to the proposition that all men are created
equal.*

*Now we are engaged in a great civil war. . .
testing whether that nation, or any nation
so conceived and so dedicated. . . can long
endure. We are met on a great battlefield
of that war.*

We have come to dedicate a portion of that field as a final resting place for those who here gave their lives that that nation might live. It is altogether fitting and proper that we should do this.

But, in a larger sense, we cannot dedicate. . . we cannot consecrate. . . we cannot hallow this ground. The brave men, living and dead, who struggled here have consecrated it, far above our poor power to add or detract. The world will little note, nor long remember, what we say here, but it can never forget what they did here.

It is for us the living, rather, to be dedicated here to the unfinished work which they who fought here have thus far so nobly advanced. It is rather for us to be here dedicated to the great task remaining before us . . .that from these honored dead we take increased devotion to that cause for which they gave the last full measure of devotion. . .that we here highly resolve that these dead shall not have died in vain. . .that this nation, under God, shall have a new birth of freedom. . . and that government of the people. . . by the people. . . for the people. . . shall not perish from the earth.

Yes, there is hope.

Who Can Lead Us?

Today, who is it that can lead this "One Nation, Indivisible, Under God" out of the darkness? Regardless of one's personal cultural avenue to God, I turn to the Old Testament for advise to those elected to positions of leadership. In II Chronicles, Chapter one, verses 9-12, the newly appointed King Solomon speaks to God:

> . . . *You have made me King over a people who are as numerous as the dust of the earth. Give me wisdom and knowledge that I may lead this people, for who is able to govern this great people of yours?*

God's answer to Solomon:

> *Since this is your heart's desire and you have not asked for wealth, riches or honor, nor for the death of your enemies and since you have not asked for a long life but for wisdom and knowledge to govern my people. . . therefore, wisdom and knowledge will be given to you.*

So, did God, even in those early times, want us to kill our enemies? It just appears that from this early time, God states that He will give wisdom and knowledge to leaders to find a different way; and then, perhaps, the teachings of Christ carry that message still further–that we should use love for all peoples to influence goodness in all.

It is clear what God expects of our leaders and citizens of this blessed country—to take the lead in efforts to erase hunger, disease and poverty at home and around the world. Americans, for the most part, both rich and poor, are full of goodness, but their efforts are made difficult when our nation's policy-makers fail to listen to other leaders.

Knowledge without wisdom lacks common sense.

So, today, in a nation united "under God", what is the place for all those churches, synagogues, mosques, shrines and temples when we know that it is our bodies that are the true "temples of God". I suggest that we consider them in this way: that, just as with the various tribes of our original Americans, the various religious organizations be considered the same way–each an organization of tribal members practicing their beliefs in different ways, but as with those early tribal Americans, all share one thread of belief and that is "in God" without argument.

I believe that today, God is crying as He patiently waits for leaders of nations to consider truth and wisdom in all aspects of leadership.

If we truly are "One Nation Under God", the time is now to live in peace with our neighbors as we discover new places of His creation, just as America was unknown to others hundreds of years ago.

So, when will the power*ful* decide to listen to the power*less* who speak with truth and wisdom?

Summary

As a Christian, of course, I thank God every day for sending his son, Jesus Christ, to teach us how to live a meaningful life. His teachings guide me to love and respect all of God's creatures, to show love to all peoples including those who are from different cultures, and to spend my energies in doing good and meeting God's needs for all people as much as I am able.

In this book, I describe two immense tragedies that resulted when peace-loving inhabitants of lands welcomed newcomers and were willing to share, but were run off their lands through dishonest treaties with the full support of religious zealots within government. Their people were destroyed while the world stood by and failed to listen to the spiritual goodness of those people—a tragic part of American history. I cannot help but wonder how many innocent lives could have been saved had the Power*ful* bothered to listen to truth and wisdom of the Power*less* and worked together for peace and dignity for all peoples.

It is no doubt that language was a problem during the early years of European immigration to this country;

however, history speaks of some who found a way through the use of body language, eye contact, and hand signs to communicate successfully for peace that most surely came from wisdom. Shamefully, promises were broken by the power*ful* who lacked wisdom.

The generosity of American Corporations and private citizens to meet the needs of the power*less* both at home and abroad, goes unrecognized by many in the world as their goodness is overshadowed by the arrogance and misguided activities of those ln power. When our elected leaders lack the courage to do what is just and right for the good of all, our Nation will continue to disappoint God and, as a result, will be of no significance to the rest of the world. Non-government entities use their assets to meet God's needs for people around the world and in the true American spirit that all things be done from the "goodness of the heart".

Of course, there is hope that change will happen. Despite their situations, the descendants of the Great Indian Chiefs and Father Chacour choose to help their people, encouraging goodness and moving a culture of "Hopelessness" to one of "Hope". Sadly, political leaders of nations, lacking wisdom, continue their agendas for power and control, resulting in the death of thousands of innocent good people all over the world.

It is with heavy heart and love that I undertook this examination of human perceptions of God. I have much sadness for where our technical world is taking our young generations. Yes, God gave us talents to discover new things he put in place at creation, just waiting to be discovered. As stated in the book of Ecclesiastes, Chapter 1, Verses 9-10.

> *What has been will be again.*
> *What has been done will be done again*
> *There is nothing new under the sun.*
>
> *Is there anything of which one can say,*
> *"Look! This is something new"?*
> *It was here already, long ago;*
> *It was here before our time.*

What we think is new, has always been, according to the wisdom of King Solomon. My disappointment is seeing our young people use wonderful discoveries as escapes from the realities of life, from creative thoughts and spirituality. They are "tied" to noise, entertainment, and computers every waking hour. In an effort to keep their bodies healthy and strong, I see them out jogging and running, ears plugged with recorded human sounds. Because of this, no new or original thoughts can enter minds or souls and the health they are seeking is weak, for it is the totality of mind, body and soul working in tandem that enables us to live our lives with purpose. I challenge our young to turn their "supposedly" disciplined exercise routine into one of total health; walk out the door, take a deep breath and allow the mind to wander.

Surely God knows we are busy, for he made us to be that way when he gave us purpose. All he expects of us is that we honor him and of course, "love our neighbors as ourselves". So simple a thing to please him; begin each day acknowledging his presence and asking for his guidance and end each day with thankfulness! That's not asking much, is it?

Epilogue

I began this book by asking my Readers to go outside in complete darkness, look up at the stars and imagine how God's Creation appeared to the ancients. My Dad's father and grandfather both were cowboys, living most of their lives "under the stars". Their spirituality continued in my father with his love and curiosity of the heavens.

My father's nightly bed-time ritual found him walking outside, looking up at the stars, taking a deep breath with peace in his heart. I believe this was his way of connecting with God and his ancestors.

During the summertime, he would beckon all to the back yard where we would lie down, look up at the stars, speak softly to each other but mostly lie in silence, enjoying the peace that the heavens above would bring—quiet time to meditate, to absorb new thoughts!

Now, I know that few will read my words, for they are written by one who represents the power*less* for I have no money with which to sell my thoughts. But then, my heart drives me to try. I am sure that my Readers have found themselves in the company of the power*ful*, perhaps at a social gathering, in which they espouse their personal views and the power*less* attempt to add to the conversation but are rudely interrupted and would simply "give up". So, why write? Why bother? Again I go back to my father who was very wise but very soft-spoken. His manner of discipline for us children was never loud, never condescending. Instead, we would find tacked to our bedroom door, a very brief message to which we could not interrupt and of course, our curiosity would cause us to read to the end. Thus, we would never disappoint our father, for his discipline was kind and to the point. So, it is my hope that this little book will be read by some of the power*ful* and inspire them to seek wisdom in all that they do.

To My Readers

Thank you for your interest in my book. I hope you will visit my web page below and share your thoughts with me.

www.culturalspirituality.com

References

American Friends Service Committee: Profiles for Peace.

Barker, Kenneth, Ed.: The New International Study Bible. Zondervan Bible Publishers, Grand Rapids, Michigan, 1985.

Barthel, Manfred: What the Bible Really Says: A Reader's Guide to the Old and New Testaments. Wings Books, New York, 1980.

Brand, Max: The Thunder Moon Series. University of Nebraska Press, Lincoln and London, 1996.

Chacour, Elias: Blood Brothers: A Palestinian Struggles for Reconciliation in the Middle East. Chosen Books. Grand Rapids, Michigan, 1939..

McMaster, Gerald and Trafzer, Clifford, Eds: Native Universe: Voices of Indian America. Smithsonian National Museum of the American Indian in association with National Geographic. Washington, DC.

Noor, Queen: Leap of Faith: Memoirs of an Unexpected Life. Miramax Books, New York 2003.

Pagels, Elaine: Beyond Belief: The Secret Gospel of Thomas. Random House, New York 2003.

Patton, Patty Sue: Eternal Threads: A Journey Towards Discovery. Authorhouse, Bloomington, Indiana, 2005.

Paul, Daniel N.: We Were Not the Savages: First Nation History, 3rd Edition. Fernwood Publishing Co., Limited, Canada.

Sennott, Charles M.: The Body and the Blood: The Holy Land's Christians at the Turn of a New Millennium. Public Affairs, New York, 2001.

The Denver Post, November 11-13, 2007. Denver, Colorado.

About the Author

Born in Muskogee, Oklahoma, she moved to Wichita Falls, Texas at about age two where she lived throughout her childhood and early marriage. Following her husband in his career in Scouting, she moved first to Vernon, Texas; then to Stillwater, Oklahoma; then to Huntsville, Texas; and finally to Houston where she retired from Baylor College of Medicine in 1987 and moved to Pagosa Springs, Colorado.

Following retirement to Pagosa Springs, she served as a volunteer teacher's assistant at the Elementary School for 10 years; served as an EMT on the ambulance service for 12 years, and currently serves as a volunteer with the Archuleta County Victims' Assistance Service for which, in 2005, she was named the "Outstanding Volunteer Advocate" for the State of Colorado.

In addition to her husband of 60 years, she is the mother of two daughters, one son, 8 grandchildren and 4 great-grandchildren.